This book is dedicated to Lettie. Remember how the mailman loved our chocolate-chip cookies?

Edited by Aileen Andres Sox
Designed by Dennis Ferree
Art by Mary Rumford
Typeset in 14/18 Weiss

Copyright © 1993 by
Pacific Press® Publishing Association
Printed in the United States of America
All rights Reserved

ISBN: 0-8163-1122-6

98 99 00 01 02 ● 5 4 3 2

Cookies in the Mailbox

By Linda Porter Carlyle   Illustrated by Mary Rumford

Pacific Press® Publishing Association
Nampa, Idaho
Oshawa, Ontario, Canada

am sitting in the shadows on the porch. I am watching and waiting. I am waiting for Mr. Hennessy.

Mr. Hennessy is one of my oldest friends. Mama says he has delivered mail on our street for twenty-four years.

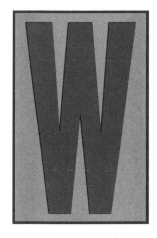hen I was little, I thought Mr. Hennessy brought me here to live with Mama and Papa. I thought he brought me in a box with a big pink bow. One day I asked Mama if that was what happened. She hugged me and laughed. "No. Mr. Hennessy only delivers mail, not babies," she said.

oday, Mr. Hennessy will be surprised. I put two cookies and a little glass of milk inside our mailbox. When he opens the box to put in the mail, he will find the surprise.

Here he comes. I see him walking along the sidewalk in the sunshine. He walks quickly. He carries a big brown bag full of letters. He has letters in his hands too.

r. Hennessy opens our mailbox and starts to put our letters inside. When he sees the cookies and milk, he smiles and says loudly, "Now what kind person had the happy thought of giving this old, tired mailman milk and cookies?" I giggle from the shadows on the porch.

Mr. Hennessy drinks the milk and wipes his mouth with the back of his hand. He puts one cookie in his mouth and one in his shirt pocket. "Thank you, kind person," he says, and waves toward the porch.

jump up and wave back. "You're welcome," I call.

ere is the mail, Mama."

Mama shakes the dishwater from her hands and dries them on a towel. "Let's see what we got today," she says. She takes the mail from me. "Bill . . . bill . . .," she mutters as she sorts the envelopes. "Oh, good! A letter from Aunt Charlotte! Let's go read it."

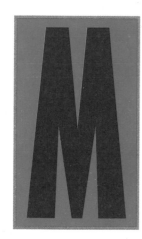

Mama and I sit on the couch together. She reads me the news from Aunt Charlotte's letter. The cousins are doing well in school. Grandma has a little cold. Someone hit Uncle Raymond's car in the parking lot of the 7-Eleven store. Uncle Tim is thinking about getting married.

Mama and I sit together and talk about our family. Mama says letters are important. They help us keep in touch with people we can't see very often.

ou know what?" asks Mama. She leans over and picks up her Bible. "This is a letter too," she says. "It's also a letter about our family. It's a letter from God, our Father, and it tells us about some of our family who lived a long time ago."

"Mama, do you mean the people in the Bible stories are my family, just like Aunt Charlotte and Uncle Raymond and Grandma?"

"Well, yes," she answers. "You know that God created the first people, Adam and Eve. And they had children who grew up and had children, and their children had children, and their children had children, and on and on. And here you are today!"

sit very still and stare at the scruffy toes of my sneakers. I am thinking about the people in the Bible stories that Mama reads to me. "Mama! Does that mean Jesus is my cousin?" I ask.

Mama smiles down at me. "No," she says, "Jesus is even closer to you than that. God's letter, the Bible, tells us He is our Brother. And God's letter tells us all about our Brother Jesus. It tells us how He loves us and came to save us. And how He will come back and take us home with Him to heaven. That's what God's letter to us is all about."

am sitting in the shadows on the porch. I can see a robin hop and stop and hop and stop across the grass. I have my Bible in my lap. I can't read all the words in it yet. Mama says "Don't worry." Pretty soon I will be able to read them all. And in the meantime, she will read God's letter to me. We will keep in touch with God, our Father, and our Brother, Jesus.

 od says, "Put My words in your heart. Put My words in your mind. Talk about them every day, when you work and when you play." (Adapted from Deuteronomy 11:18,19.)

Parent's Guide

Share Your Love of God's Word With Your Child

You can help your child associate the words and stories in the Bible as personal messages from God by implementing the following ideas into your family life:

❖ Give your child his own Bible. Choose from the beginner's type of Bible at first. (These are Bible stories, rather than actual Scripture.) Have your child bring you his Bible and read from it at each worship.

❖ When your child is a little older, help her pick out a "big kid's" Bible. There are translations of the whole Bible done on a third-grade reading level so a child of four or five years of age can understand and appreciate it in small doses. Let your child read to you as she learns how to read. (If you are a new Christian who does not know where to look for Bible stories, the picture pages in these translations often tell the Scripture passage.)

❖ Refer to the Bible as God's Word to us or His letter to us.

❖ As your child can understand, talk about how the Bible came to us—how God influenced people to write it, copy it, preserve it, translate it, and share it. Your local Christian bookstore can tell you about books to help you tell your child this story.

❖ Memorize Scripture in your home. One good way to do this is through Scripture songs, many of which have been written and recorded. If you're musically gifted, make up a few songs yourself.

Or sing Bible verses to the tunes of other songs.

❖ When you tell a Bible story, show where you find the story in the Bible so that your child associates the story with its source.

❖ Be sure your child knows that the stories in the Bible are about real people who really did these things. Help her differentiate between the true stories of the Bible and the made-up stories she may watch on television or read in other books.

❖ Use caution in your choice of Bible videos. Some of these videos tell the Bible story in such a way that a child cannot know what really happened in the Bible story and what is the fictional part of the video. Small children, especially, regard what they are seeing as true.

❖ Let your child see you studying and treasuring your Bible, turning to it in times of great need, relying on its wisdom, applying its teaching to your daily life. As you do this in your home, your child will come to know and rely on this personal revelation of our Redeemer and Creator.

Linda Porter Carlyle and Aileen Andres Sox

Books by Linda Porter Carlyle

I Can Choose
A Child's Steps to Jesus

God and Joseph and Me   *Cookies in the Mailbox*
Rescued From the River!   *Beautiful Bones and Butterflies*
Grandma Stepped on Fred!   *No Olives Tonight!*
Max Moves In   *Happy Birthday Tomorrow to Me!*